Rails Through The Heart of Wales

The Heart of Wales Line 150 Years on

G.P. Essex

Albion Books

First edition 2018 by Albion Books

Copyright G.P.Essex

www.scenebyrail.com

All photos by the author unless otherwise stated.
For picture credits see page 62

All rights reserved No part of this publication may be reproduced, stored in a retrieval system or transmitted in any form or by any means without the prior permission of the copyright holder.

The right of G. P. Essex to be identified as the author of this work has been asserted by him in accordance with the
Copyright Designs and Patents Act 1988

Printed by Barrington Print, Leominster

Albion Books, 10 Corn Square, Leominster. HR6 8LR
www.albionbooks.co.uk

ISBN 9781916449800

The author would like to thank (in no particular order)

Hayley Philips, Anthony Birdwood, Jon Critchley, Mike Evans, Joan Snaith, Richard Rees, Rachel Francis, Stephen Thomas, HOWLTA, Parry Bryony, Jennifer Bollen Dorian SPencer Davies, Emyr Evans, Lizzie Fotheringham, Rob the Gwilli signalman, Nigel and Sue at Nigel Bird Books, The National Library of Wales, The Radnorshire Society, Network Rail, The Gwilli Railway, The Severn Valley Railway, Geoff Marshall and Vicki Pipe from All The Stations.
Any anyone else I can't think of right now...

Cover photograph: Sugar Loaf Summit

Contents

Introduction & statistics	5
Timeline	6
Maps	8
History	10
The Railway at Builth Road	21
The Glanrhyd Bridge Disaster	26
A journey along the line	29
The Railway Today	51
A brighter future?	53
Station Useage statistics	54
More Than Numbers	55
Transport For Wales	56
Heart Of Wales Line Development Co	58
Heart Of Wales Line Trail	59
HOWLTA	60
Further Resources	61
Bibliography & Credits	62

Above: Black Five' 4-6-0 45407 The Lancashire Fusilier (masquerading as 45157 Glasgow Yeomanry) & BR 4MT 2-6-0 76079 near Llangunlo with the The Central Wales Explorer, on 19th April 2008. *Mike Evans*

Below: Arriva class 142 on Knucklas Viaduct.

Introduction.

The Heart of Wales Line, also known as the Central Wales Line is an unusual and fascinating railway. Its chequered 150 year history has taken it from a multi ownership line with hundreds of staff at its 32 stations, to a shadow of its former self, as the longest "light railway" in Britain, albeit one with a promising future.

This book aims to give an insight and guide into the history of the line, its future, and the community that supports it. But don't just take my word for it, get on the train and enjoy the journey!

Heart of Wales Line Statistics

Length	121 Miles
Stations	32
Closed stations	6
Tunnels	5
Bridges	191
Level Crossings	13
User Worked ('farm') crossings*	67
Viaducts	2
Passing Loops	5
Request Stops	22
Route Availability	5

* *User worked ('farm') crossings are the most common crossing on the railway network - about 2/3 of the total, They are either a basic footpath crossing; a crossing with gates and instructional signage; or a crossing with a telephone to the nearest signalbox, where users must call first before crossing.*

A Timeline of events.

1859	Central Wales Railway founded (Knighton to Llandrindod)
1860	Central Wales Extension Railway founded (Llandrindod to Llandovery)
1861	Bucknell to Knighton opened, Knighton to Knucklas opened for freight
1862	LNWR/GWR joint lease of Shrewsbury to Craven Arms (Hereford) route. Passenger traffic to Knucklas opened
1865	Central Wales Railway extended to Llandrindod
1866	Central Wales Extension Railway opened Llandrindod to Builth Road High Level
1867	Central Wales Extension Railway opened Builth Road to LLanwrtyd
1868	Central Wales Extension Railway opened Llandrindod to Llandovery. Knighton Railway, CWR and CWER taken over by LNWR.
1870	LNWR/GWR joint ownership of Shrewsbury to Craven Arms (Hereford) route.
1871	Llanelly Railways Portardulais to Swansea line transferred to a separate company owned by the LNWR
1889	Llaenelly Railway and Dock Co taken over by GWR
1911	Llanelly riots. Army response to railway strike leaves 5 civilians dead.
1923	LWNR absorbed into London Midland and Scottish Railway
1948	Nationalisation The whole line comes under the control of British Rail (Western Region)
1949	Roof collapse in Sugar Loaf tunnel
1952	Queen Elizabeth II sets foot in Wales for the first time as Queen at Llandridod Wells station, to open the Claerwen Dam
1955	Queen Elizabeth II arrives by train at Llandovery station when opening Usk reservoir
1962	Threat of closure, BR proposes closing the line, or providing a much reduced service. Builth Road Low Level closed
1964	Portardulais to Swansea Victoria route closed. DMU service Llanelli to Shrewsbury. Through freight rerouted
1965	Sugar Loaf station closes. Line downgraded to single track.
1967	Another threat of closure
1970	Reprieve. Through trains Shrewsbury to Swansea High Street Station (via Llanelli) announced

1972	Pantyffynnon to Craven Arms reclassified as a Light Railway
1980	Heavy locomotives banned on the line.
1980	Cilycwn Road bridge replaced after lorry strike
1981	Heart of Wales Line Travellers Association (HOWLTA) formed
1983	Dolau Station Action Group founded
1984	Sugar Loaf Station reopens
1985	£600,000 investment announced
1986	Signalling system modernised and redesigned. Pantyffynnon signal box now controlling line as far as Craven Arms
1987	Glanrhyd Bridge Disaster. Llandeilo to Llandovery temporarily closed
1988	Glanrhyd Bridge reinstated. Llandeilo to Llandovery services resume.
1989	Return of excursion trains after heavy locomotive ban lifted
1990	Knighton passing loop restored, Llandrindod station canopy replaced and signal box moved and reopened as a museum
1991	Central Wales Line Forum founded
1993	Celebrations of the 125th Anniversary of the line opening. Summertime steam special services begin.
1994	Privatisation. Railtrack Plc takes control of track and infrastructure, Trains operated by South Wales and West.
1996	Rolling stock purchased by ROSCO. Prism Rail Plc awarded franchise for operating the line
1997	£300,000 budget for station repairs and improvements
2002	The Queen & Prince Philip visit Dolau station
2003	Arriva Wales awarded franchise
2010	£5 million improvements to passing loops and infrastructure
2011	Prince Charles reopens the newly restored Llandovery station
2016	Llandeilo station community hub opened. Pantyffynnon station building refurbished
2017	£3.5 million Cynhorgy viaduct restoration completed
2018	Keolis Amey awarded franchise, branded as Transport for Wales (TFW)

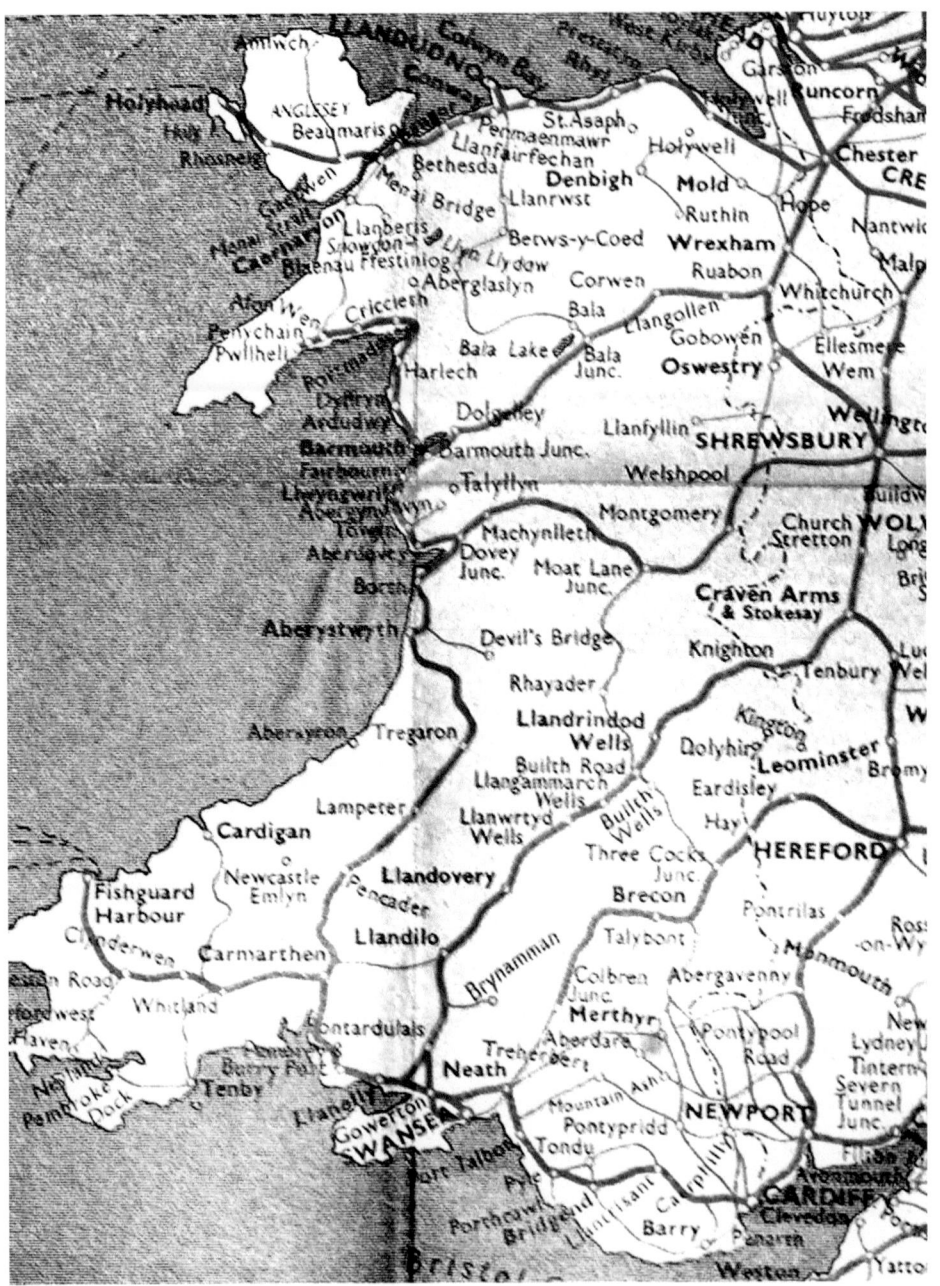

Above: The network of lines that once crossed Wales is shown in this 1958 British Rail map, just before Beeching shredded it.

Right: The Heart of Wales line, with surrounding lines today

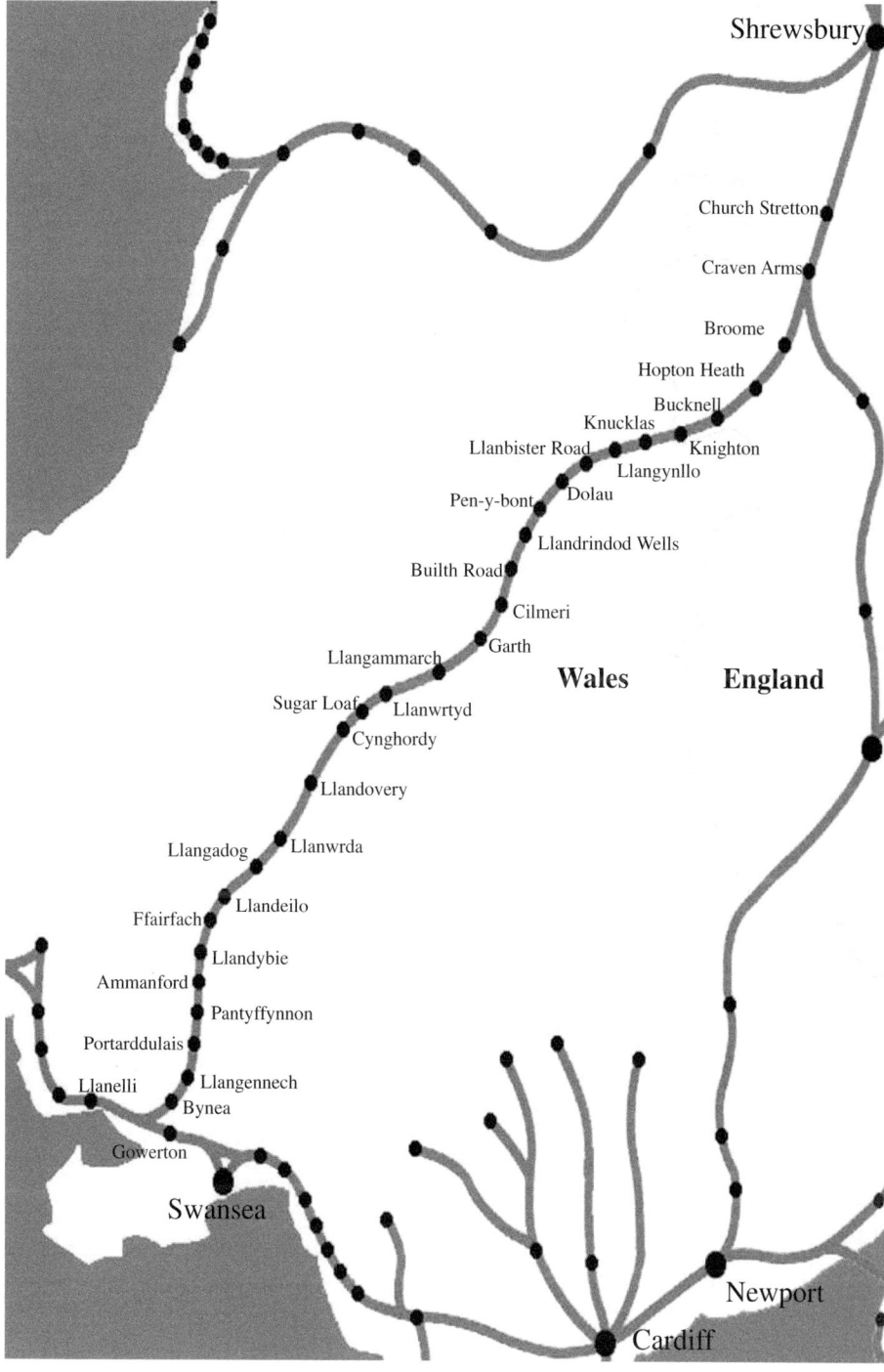

A brief history

The line was formerly known as the Central Wales line, and still is by some railway staff. The name Heart of Wales Line was adopted in 1980 to help with promoting the line for tourism.

Originally intended to link industrial South Wales with the Midlands and Manchester, the line was built in stages by a series of small private companies.

The Llanelly Railway and Dock Company was established in 1828 and its first line was a horse-drawn colliery line between Dafen and Llanelli. This was followed some years later by the Llanelli to Pontarddulais line, opened in 1839, which is now the southernmost part of the Heart of Wales route. Construction continued in stages, reaching Pantyffynon in 1840 and Tirydail (now Ammanford) in 1841 and finally Llandeilo in 1857.

Meanwhile the Vale of Towey Railway, founded in 1854, opened a line from Llandeilo to Llandovery in 1858, leasing it to the Llanelly Railway and Dock Company. In the north, the Hereford and Shrewsbury Railway had gone as far as Craven Arms, where the station opened in 1851.

There were three companies that developed the line through Shropshire, Radnorshire and Brecknockshire which would connect Llandovery with Craven Arms. The Knighton Railway, the Central Wales Railway, and the Central Wales Extension Railway.

> **THE CENTRAL WALES RAILWAY.**
>
> On Friday last the Government Inspector went over that portion of the line which has just been completed, and was perfectly satisfied with the manner in which the work has been done. This is most creditable to all concerned in the undertaking. The line was opened through for goods and minerals on Monday last, and on Monday next it will be opened for passengers. We have now direct narrow-gauge communication with Liverpool, Manchester, Birmingham, and other large towns. The fares are exceedingly low, and the service of trains announced in another column meet the requirements of the country at present. Important alterations have been made in the time-table of the Llanelly lines which we did not know of soon enough to insert in our eighth page. They appear, however, in an advertisement in our fourth page. We call particular attention to that advertisement and also to the advertisement of the London and North Western Railway.
>
> Article in "The Welshman" June 1868

> ‡"Twice a day at Talley Road, milk from six farms would arrive in milk churns, to be loaded on the down GWR to Llanelli and hence to Paddington. The morning milk would be despatched on the 9am down, the evening milk went on the 7pm down, and the empties collected. This pattern of milk collections happened on most stations of the line before the days of milk tankers‡".
>
> C Boyd.

The Knighton Railway was incorporated by Act of Parliament in 1858 and proceeded to build the 12 ½ mile line from Craven Arms. Bad weather was blamed for the length of time it took to complete. The first part, 9 miles from Craven Arms to Bucknell, opened in October 1860, the final 3 miles to Knighton opened in March 1861.

The Central Wales Railway was incorporated in August 1859 to take the line the 20 miles from Knighton as far as Llandrindod, to terminate at or near the Llanerch Inn "near Llandrindod". It took 5 years to complete and ran into financial difficulties, including a legal dispute between contractor and company over costs.

The first 2 miles as far as Knucklas opened for mineral traffic only in 1861 and for passengers the following year. In 1863 the Central Wales Railway, which already had very close links with the Knighton Railway, was amalgamated with the latter by an Act of Parliament.

The next section of the line, 17 miles as far as Penybont (originally known as Cross Gates) opened in 1864. Finally, Penybont to Llandrindod was completed in 1865. This section was officially opened on 10th October 1865.

The final link between the various lines was the Central Wales Extension Railway, incorporated by an Act of Parliament in July 1860 to take the line the final 26 miles to Llandovery. It was completed in four sections with construction starting the same year, and the final section being completed in June 1868. The most difficult section proved to be between Llanwrtyd and Llandovery, with Sugar Loaf tunnel giving many problems.

The 1000-yard tunnel had various areas of unsound rock and a large body of water in the centre, and some sections soon had to be relined after being found to be unsafe. Meanwhile the Cynghordy viaduct had to have a change of contactors and its foundations relined part way through construction, which, in total cost over £15,000.

The formal opening was on 8th October 1868, six years later than expected, and by this time the London and North Western Railway (LNWR) had absorbed all three of the original companies, which were primarily concerned with getting the lines built and had no real interest in the day-to-day running of services.

Cynghordy Station c. 1900. D Harries, NLW

LLandeilo Station, WW1, Waiting for a troop train. D Harries NLW

The LNWR shared the Vale of Towy Railway with the Llanelly Railway, who, in 1867, opened a line to connect Pontardulais with Swansea Victoria.

In 1871 the LNWR won a legal battle to give it control of the Vale of Towy line, and in 1889 the rest of the Llanelly Railway's interests were absorbed by the Great Western Railway (GWR).

By this time the line was being jointly run by the GWR and LNWR in various sections, with Shrewsbury to Craven Arms and Llandovery to Llandeilo being jointly operated. The Llandeilo to Llanelli section was owned by the GWR but with LNWR running powers, and the LNWR owned and operated the Craven Arms to Llandovery and Pontardulais to Swansea Victoria sections.

Eventually, double track was laid on most sections of the line, although the Knighton to Llanbister Road, Llandrindod to Pantyffynon and Pen y Bont tunnel sections have always been single track.

The railway and its surrounding towns developed and prospered, with extensive goods yards at many stations, carrying a multitude of freight, parcels and livestock. At this time, railways were "common carriers" and had to accept any freight for carriage.

On occasion whole farms were moved by rail, with a special train stopping adjacent to the farm,

G.W.R Boundary Marker, Ffairfach

G.W.R Postcard 1934
Llanwrda "Nothing Left Behind"

lineside fences removed and the whole farm, from livestock to implements, loaded onto a train and moved to its new home.

There were regular specials, daily and weekly, carrying perishable and high priority goods, such as the daily "York Mail" which was followed by the "fish train", which started at Swansea and collected more wagons at Milford Haven and Llandeilo Junction before heading to Crewe and the north.

In the late 19th Century, a little known proposal to supply London with water almost had a drastic effect on the line, with plans to divert it around the massive scheme.

Had the plan gone ahead, it would have submerged the villages of Garth and Llangammarch under the Irfon reservoir, one of seven that would have displaced thousands of residents and had a dramatic effect on Mid Wales. Fortunately the scheme was dropped at the last moment, with the preferred option of abstracting and treating water from the River Thames.

"I was a guard at Shrewsbury for many years and the Central Wales Line was my favourite run back in the steam days, when Knighton held their sheep sales. I have left Shrewsbury at about 5am with an engine and brake van for Llanbister Road where we would attach loaded wagons of sheep then proceed to Dolau, attach more wagons of sheep and form the train ready to return to Knighton.
The engine had to go to Penybont to run round the train, the farmers used to ride in the brake van with us to Knighton. The sheep were unloaded and taken to the market by the farmers, we then used to stay at Knighton with the engine and assist with shunting until we were relieved, at that time Mr Davies was the Station Master at Knighton".
H Morgan

Llanelli was the scene of serious rioting in 1911 as a result of picketing action during the National Railway strike. A crowd of about 2000 people gathered at the station and attempted to prevent the movement of a train carrying strike-breaking workers. This led to the reading of the Riot Act by the local Justices and troops opened fire towards the crowd. Two young men were killed by the gunfire and the crowds rioted through the town for 12 hours, causing widespread devastation. Four more people died as a result of an exploding munitions wagon. Today the riots are mostly forgotten, and there is no memorial or any commemorations in the town.

Moving on to 1923, with the grouping of the railways into the "big four" the LNWR became part of the London, Midland and Scottish Railway (LMS) as a result of the 1921 Railways Act. The GWR, being the only railway company to survive the grouping, retained control of the line between Llandeilo and Pontarddulais. During the pre-war years various improvement schemes to the surrounding lines were abandoned, and Grovesend station on the Gowerton line was closed in 1932. Some other stations suffered a reduction in services and facilities, with Glanrhyd being relegated to an unstaffed halt in 1938, and Talley Road suffering the same fate in 1941.

Timetable, The Welshman Newspaper, November 1868

During this period the services consisted of five LMS passenger trains a day between Swansea and Shrewsbury, some of which contained through coaches for Liverpool, Manchester, Birmingham and York. In addition there were frequent local services between Pontarddulais and Swansea, including some Sunday services.

The line suffered, along with the rest of Britain's railways, during the Second World War. Swansea Victoria was damaged by bombing, including the roof, which was never fully repaired. A Royal Ordnance factory at Crofty on the Gower brought additional traffic, as did the hospital trains heading for the military hospital at Credenhill, along with regular troop trains and military freight.

After the railways were nationalised in 1948, the line passed to the control of the Western Region of British Railways. This caused some displeasure amongst the predominantly LNWR/LMS staff on the line, which was reinforced by the changes to locomotive allocations. Former LNWR engines were replaced with LMS engines, including Black 5's and Stanier class 2's, along with GWR pannier tanks.

In the late 1950s diesel railcars built at Swindon were introduced. Services throughout the 1950s saw passenger and freight traffic decline, resulting in the closure of Derydd Road station in 1954, with Parcyrhun Halt, Talley Road and Glanrhyd following in 1955.

DOWN TRAINS.			A	B		
	p.m.	a.m.	a.m.	a.m.	noon.	
London(Euston-sq.)dep.	9 0	..	..	9 0	12 0	
Northampton	10 15	..	..	..	1 15	
Rugby	11 17	..	..	11 5	2 15	
Leicester	8 35	..	..	11 40	11 40	
Birmingham (New-st.)	10 30	..	7 45	11 5	1 45	
Wolverhampton (Queen street.)	11 0	..	8 20	11 40	2 24	
Stafford	2 13	..	8 53	12 30	3 56	
Shrewsbury arr.	3 5	..	10 15	1 30	5 0	
				p.m.		
Edinburgh dep.	4 15	..	9 30	..	..	
Glasgow	4 0	..	9 10	..	..	
			a.m.			
Carlisle	7 50	..	12 47	..	9 0	
Preston	11 14	..	6 15	9 25	12 10	
Liverpool (Lime-st.)	11 15	..	7 30	10 15	12 50	
Leeds	9 30	..	..	7 50	11 0	
Bradford	10 0	..	..	5 45	9 40	
Halifax	10 0	..	..	6 0	..	
Huddersfield	11 7	..	..	8 30	12 5	
Manchester (Lond.-rd.)	10 55	..	7 45	10 45	1 30	
Stockport	12 12	..	7 58	11 5	1 54	
Chester	11 6	..	..	9 25	2 0	
Crewe	1 8	..	9 0	12 30	3 40	
Shrewsbury arr.	3 5	..	10 15	1 35	4 55	
Shrewsbury dep.	..	7 0	10 25	1 45	5 10	
Craven Arms	..	8 5	11 15	2 30	6 15	
Knighton	..	8 35	11 45	3 0	6 45	
Llandrindod Wells	..	..	9 33	12 40	3 55	7 42
Worcester dep.	......	....	....	11 0	2 0	
Hereford	......	....	....	12 45	4 0	
Brecon	......	7 15	....	1 15	5 10	
Builth	......	8 20	....	2 20	6 13	
Builth Road arr.	......	8 23	....	2 25	6 16	
Llanidloes dep.	......	7 15	11 45	..	4 25	
Builth Road	......	8 15	12 52	..	5 33	
Builth Road dep.	......	9 56	12 52	4 10	7 57	
Llanwrtyd Wells	......	10 21	1 17	4 35	8 27	
Cynhordy	......	10 34	......	—	8 42	
Llandovery arr.	......	10 50	1 40	5 0	8 57	
Llandovery dep.	......	11 0	1 45	5 10	9 5	
Llandilo arr.	......	11 28	2 10	5 37	9 30	
Llandilo dep.	......	11 35	2 30	5 40	....	
Carmarthen	......	12 20	3 15	6 30	....	
Llandilo dep.	......	11 32	2 15	5 40	9 30	
Pontardulais arr.	......	12 15	2 55	6 25	10 13	
Llanelly (G.W.R. Stat.)	......	12 45	3 30	7 0	....	
Pontardulais dep.	......	12 20	2 57	6 30	10 15	
Swansea (Vic.-st.) C	......	12 50	3 30	7 0	10 45	

RETURN TICKETS

From Swansea, Llanelly, and Carmarthen to Shrewsbury and Crewe will be available for Three Days; and to London, Liverpool, Manchester, and Warrington for Four Days.

In 1962 British Railways (BR) applied to close the line, but the Ministry of Transport refused after receiving several objections, and agreed to a number of reductions in the service level, implemented in 1964.

The Swansea Victoria to Pontarddulais section was closed, with services terminating at Llanelli, with DMUs now making four journeys each way instead of the previous five per day. During the next few years many goods yards closed, with mineral traffic at the southern end of the line making up the majority of the freight traffic.

15

Again in 1967 BR applied to close the line entirely, and it almost succeeded. The story goes that the Secretary of State for Wales at the time, George Thomas, pointed out that the line ran through several marginal constituencies, the result being that the line received a reprieve, and an increase in grant aid!

After public pressure the service through to Swansea was reinstated in 1970, although it now reversed out of Llanelli to Swansea High Street, as it does today. Services were amended at the same time to bring the level back up to the previous five trains per day. A drive for more passengers was launched, and by May 1971 the passenger receipts were up 27%.

To minimise running costs the line received a dramatic overhaul in 1972. The section from Pantyffynon to Craven Arms was designated a Light Railway, with much simpler signalling systems, less staffing and consequently much lower running costs.
The line received a further blow in 1976 when, faced with a £1million estimate for essential repair work, BR banned loco-hauled services in an effort to prolong the track's life. This meant an end to all excursion traffic, which by now had become a regular feature of the line, with the consequential loss to businesses of the tourism trade, especially in Llandrindod Wells and Llanwrtyd.

Above: Knighton Station c. 1900-1910. P.B.Abery, NLW

Opposite. Llandovery Station bookstall, 1910. D.C. Harries, NLW

Above: Knucklas Viaduct, engraving from The Illustrated London News, 1865
Below: Llanwrtyd Wells Station c.1900

Local concerns about the line's future led to the formation of the Heart Of Wales Line Travellers' Association (HOWLTA) in 1981 as a pressure group, it has been very successful in promoting the line and campaigning for better services.

Broome Station c.1900. P.B.Abery, NLW

In 1985/6 over £600,000 was invested in the line to update the signalling system to a "No Signalman Key Token" system (NSKT), so that the signal box at Pantyffynon controls the entire 79-mile section to Craven Arms, with the drivers obtaining tokens for sections of the route in small cabins at stations, where they call the signalman to obtain permission to withdraw the token. At stations with level crossings there are also driver/guard operated controls for the crossings.

In 1990 the heavy locomotive ban was lifted, and, after some heavy criticism regarding the condition of the permanent way, BR reinstated several redundant passing loops and excursion trains resumed. In 1993 the line celebrated its 125th anniversary, with a large event in Llandovery and steam specials arriving in the town for the event.

After privatisation, services were operated by several different Train Operating Companies (TOCs). The adoption of stations by community groups continued, with a memorable visit to Dolau station by HM the Queen in 2002. Another royal visit, in 2010, by Prince Charles, marked the opening of the Llandovery Station community café, which is a thriving volunteer-run café, hosting art exhibitions, poetry evenings and model railway displays.

> "My parents ran a pub in Llandovery in the late 50's. They would send the beer order to Marston's in Burton on Trent first class in the 3pm post on Sunday. The delivery arrived at the pub at 11am Tuesday, delivered from the station".
> Joan Snaith

In recent years Network Rail has continued to upgrade and invest in the line; many of the stations now have small distinctive shelters and digital information boards, and there are plans for more improvements with the recently-awarded franchise.

Notes

c On Saturdays until 10 June and from 9 September Manchester Piccadilly arr 20.49
   On Saturdays 17 June to 2 September Manchester Piccadilly arr 19.43, Liverpool Lime Street 19.43

e On Saturdays arr 01.47

f On Saturdays dep 12.37

g On Saturdays 17 June to 2 September Manchester Piccadilly arr 15.22, Liverpool Lime Street, 15.48

Heavy figures denote through carriages; light figures denote connecting services

Note: These tables are subject to alteration

Published by British Rail (Western Region)
Printed by E. J. Day & Co Ltd

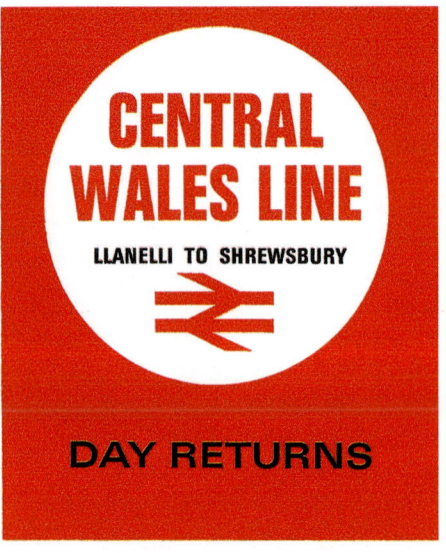

CENTRAL WALES LINE
LLANELLI TO SHREWSBURY

DAY RETURNS

Timetable and fares
6 March 1967 to 4 May 1968

Llanelli → Builth Road → Shrewsbury
Weekdays

SWANSEA HIGH STREET	05.27	09.40	14.10	18.15
LLANELLI	06.10	10.10	14.35	18.55
BYNEA HALT	06.15		14.40	
LLANGENNECH HALT	06.19		14.44	
PONTARDULAIS HALT	06.24	10.23	14.49	19.11
PANTYFFYNNON	06.32	10.31	14.57	19.20
AMMANFORD & TIRYDAIL HT.	06.36	10.34	15.00	19.24
LLANDEBIE	06.41		15.05	
FFAIRFACH HALT	06.50		15.14	
LLANDILO	06.54	10.50	15.18	19.43
LLANGADOG HALT	07.03	10.59	15.27	19.52
LLANWRDA HALT	07.07		15.31	
LLANDOVERY	07.14	11.09	15.38	20.05
CYNGHORDY	07.22		15.46	20.14
LLANWRTYD WELLS	07.35	11.29	15.58	20.32
LLANGAMMARCH WELLS	07.41	11.35	16.04	20.38
GARTH	07.45		16.08	20.42
CILMERY HALT	07.51		16.14	20.48
BUILTH ROAD H.L. HALT	**07.55**	**11.46**	**16.18**	**20.52**
LLANDRINDOD WELLS	08.06	11.58	16.29	21.06
PENYBONT HALT	08.12	12.14	16.36	21.13
DOLAU HALT	08.18	12.19	16.41	21.19
LLANBISTER ROAD	08.24	12.25	16.47	21.25
LLANGUNLLO HALT	08.29		16.53	
KNUCKLAS HALT	08.37		17.00	
KNIGHTON HALT	08.42	12.41	17.06	21.43
BUCKNELL HALT	08.49	12.47	17.12	21.49
HOPTON HEATH	08.54		17.17	
BROOME	08.59		17.22	
CRAVEN ARMS	**09.07**	**13.03**	**17.30**	**22.06**
CHURCH STRETTON	09.17	13.13	17.40	
SHREWSBURY	**09.34**	**13.30**	**17.57**	**22.33**
BIRMINGHAM (NEW STREET)	10.59	14.59	20.05	
LONDON (EUSTON)	12.51	16.50	21.50	
MANCHESTER (PICCADILLY)	12.30	15.35g	20.56c	01.27e
LIVERPOOL (LIME STREET)	12.35	15.22g	21.15c	01.31

for explanation of notes see back cover

Shrewsbury → Builth Road → Llanelli
Weekdays

LIVERPOOL (LIME STREET)	00.10	08.50	12.30f	16.30
MANCHESTER (PICCADILLY)	00.45	08.37	12.37	16.27
LONDON (EUSTON)			11.15	15.15
BIRMINGHAM (NEW STREET)		09.00	13.00	17.00
SHREWSBURY		**03.52**	**10.32**	**14.57**	**18.30**
CHURCH STRETTON			10.51	15.15	18.48
CRAVEN ARMS		**04.21**	**11.02**	**15.26**	**18.59**
BROOME			11.13	15.37	
HOPTON HEATH			11.17		19.13
BUCKNELL HALT		04.42	11.24	15.46	19.19
KNIGHTON HALT		04.52	11.31	15.53	19.27
KNUCKLAS HALT			11.36		
LLANGUNLLO HALT			11.45	16.06	19.39
LLANBISTER ROAD			11.51	16.11	19.45
DOLAU HALT			11.57	16.18	19.51
PENYBONT HALT		05.21	12.02	16.23	19.56
LLANDRINDOD WELLS		05.32	12.12	16.34	20.04
BUILTH ROAD H.L. HALT		**05.43**	**12.21**	**16.43**	**20.13**
CILMERY HALT			12.25	16.47	
GARTH			12.31	16.53	20.21
LLANGAMMARCH WELLS		05.56	12.35	16.57	20.25
LLANWRTYD WELLS		06.04	12.42	17.04	20.33
CYNGHORDY			12.53	17.15	20.44
LLANDOVERY		06.26	13.02	17.25	20.53
LLANWRDA HALT		06.33	13.09	17.31	21.00
LLANGADOG HALT		06.38	13.14	17.36	21.05
LLANDILO		06.55	13.24	17.45	21.15
FFAIRFACH HALT			13.26	17.47	
LLANDEBIE			13.36	17.57	21.25
AMMANFORD & TIRYDAIL HT.		07.11	13.41	18.02	21.30
PANTYFFYNNON		07.16	13.45	18.06	
PONTARDULAIS HALT		07.25	13.52	18.13	21.40
LLANGENNECH HALT			13.59	18.20	
BYNEA HALT			14.03	18.24	
LLANELLI		**07.40**	**14.10**	**18.30**	**21.56**
SWANSEA HIGH STREET		08.10	15.02	19.02	22.37

for explanation of notes see back cover

The Railway at Builth Road

This photo of Builth Road High Level from around 1910 shows a local freight leaving, with the goods shed in the background.. The posters advertise holidays and LNWR postcards.
The object on the platform appears to be a small canvas bag with luggage label. D.C.Harries, NLW

In its heyday Builth Road was a thriving community in its own right. The junction of the Central Wales Railway and the Mid Wales Railway was built on two different levels, with a spur linking the two. The Central Wales railway's High Level station opened for traffic in 1866.

The Mid Wales line ran from Brecon to Moat Lane Junction at Caersws. It was taken over by the Cambrian Railways in 1904, then by the GWR in 1922. Its station at Builth Road opened in 1864 on the lower level running under, and almost at right angles, to the Central Wales line.

Two rows of railway workers cottages were built by 1892, with the station master's houses there were almost 50 dwellings in the area surrounding the stations.

Although the stations were ran by separate companies until nationalisation in 1948, they had to work together in many way. In fact the 1881 census records that the Mid Wales station master was a lodger at the LNWR station master house! It is recorded that he got his own dwelling in 1893.

There was a considerable exchange of passengers, goods and mail traffic between the stations, a water powered counterweight goods lift was built in 1887 to connect the two, it can be seen in the 1960's photos. The high level station also had an extensive goods yard, with facilities for handling all manner of traffic, including a two ton yard crane.

The railways were far more self sufficient in terms of their infrastructure and equipment needs than today. Many people are aware of the large locomotive works such as Swindon and Crewe, but it is also illustrated by places such as Builth Road. Just north of the station, the River Dulais provided water for locomotives and all non-drinking purposes. The locomotive depot staff were responsible for the maintenance and operation of a steam pumping engine that extracted water from the river into a large storage tank at the goods depot.

In the triangle between the main and loop lines, the LNWR established a maintenance depot, nicknamed 'Dartmoor' (the reason for which is lost in the mists of time) which was well established by the 1890's. It employed a multitude of tradesmen, with responsibility for all the infrastructure repair and maintenance on the line between Craven Arms and Swansea.

The staffing levels illustrate the size of the operation. Including a few specialists such signal and telegraph engineers and a carriage and wagon examiner, over 70 men worked at the depot in the 1920's, in addition to the 30 or so staff employed on the stations.

Most of these were housed in railway dwellings with their families, or nearby on the Pencerrig estate. However about 20 cycled in from Builth Wells. The railway houses, which survive today in private hands, were well built, and although lacking in modern conveniences, the standard was superior to most working class dwellings of the period. They were all provided with gardens, allotments were available, and a communal bakehouse was situated behind Railway Terrace.

Builth Road High Level, B.R. Standard Class 5 73035 6th Sept 1962. Roger Joanes
This was one of the rarer class 5's fitted with Caprotti valve gear

An unidentified 2MT on the low level, the goods lift is the white structure adjacent

At the time a job on the railway, although not the best paid, was a secure job for life, with perks such as good accommodation and concessionary travel. There was a strong sense of community, with plenty of activities centred around the church and chapel congregations, a football team, and recreation room in the high level station, complete with billiard table.

However, as competition from road transport grew in the 1930's life for the railways became harder.

Builth Road 2018. Railway Terrace is on the left with the goods shed in the distance.

23

Builth Road Low Level, with Ivatt 2MT No 46516. 1962

The LMS, having taken control of the LNWR in the 1923 grouping, embarked on a period of economies, although the retirement of many Builth employees during the period meant the cutbacks were not as drastic as at other locations.

After World War Two, when fuel rationing was lifted, the surge in road transport had an even more dramatic effect, and with the Beeching axe falling heavily on Wales, the Mid Wales line closed totally in 1962. The houses were all sold to a property company in the 1960's which, in turn, sold them on to become owner occupied dwellings. At the same time the Dartmoor depot was finally closed and sold off, the land is now used as a timber yard. If you stop and take a stroll round Builth Road today there's still plenty remaining of this once thriving railway community.

Builth Road Low Level, showing the Central Wales overbridge in the background. Ivatt class 2MT 46508 is in the platform 1962 Roger Joanes

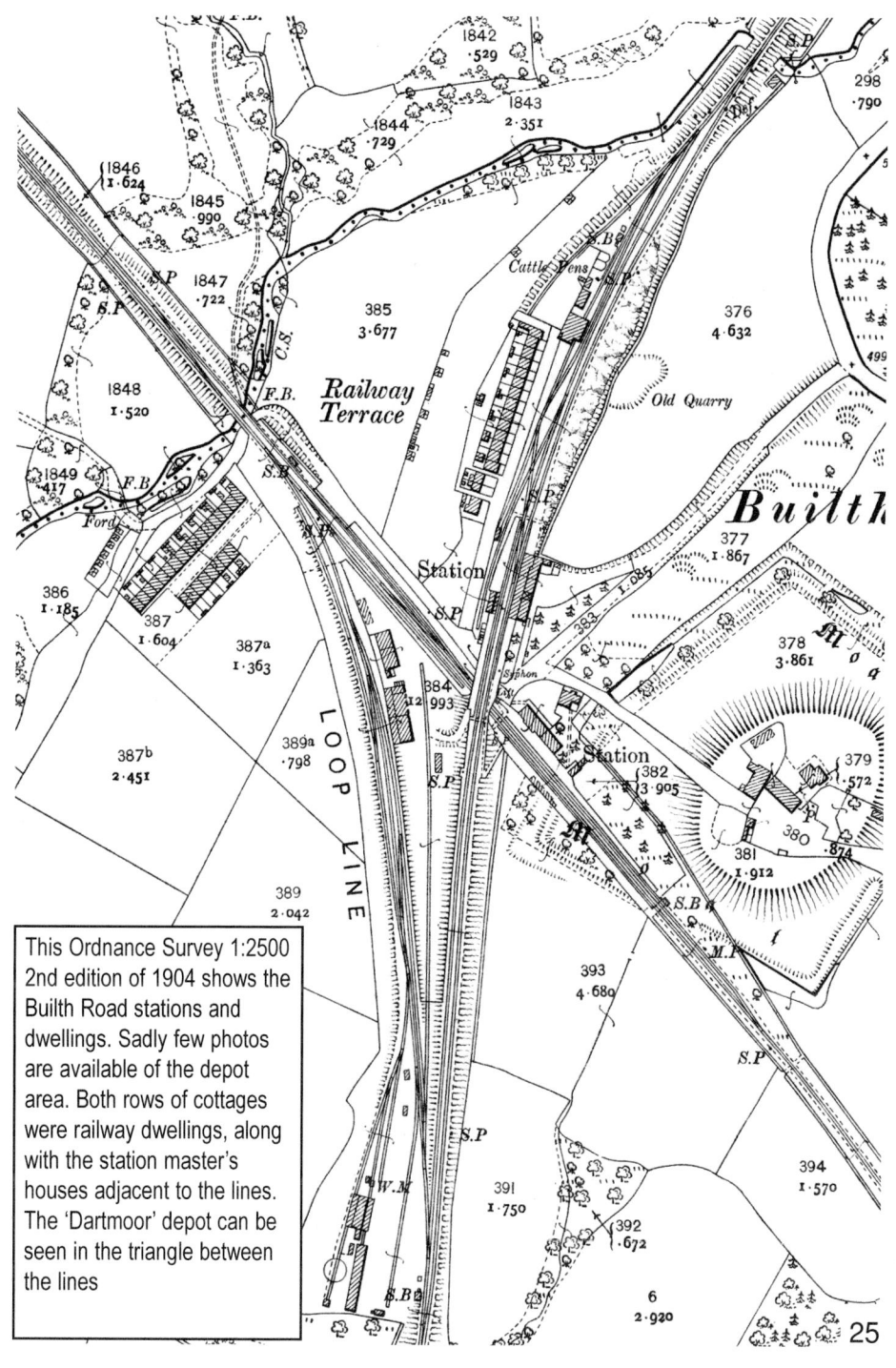

This Ordnance Survey 1:2500 2nd edition of 1904 shows the Builth Road stations and dwellings. Sadly few photos are available of the depot area. Both rows of cottages were railway dwellings, along with the station master's houses adjacent to the lines. The 'Dartmoor' depot can be seen in the triangle between the lines

The Glanrhyd Bridge Disaster

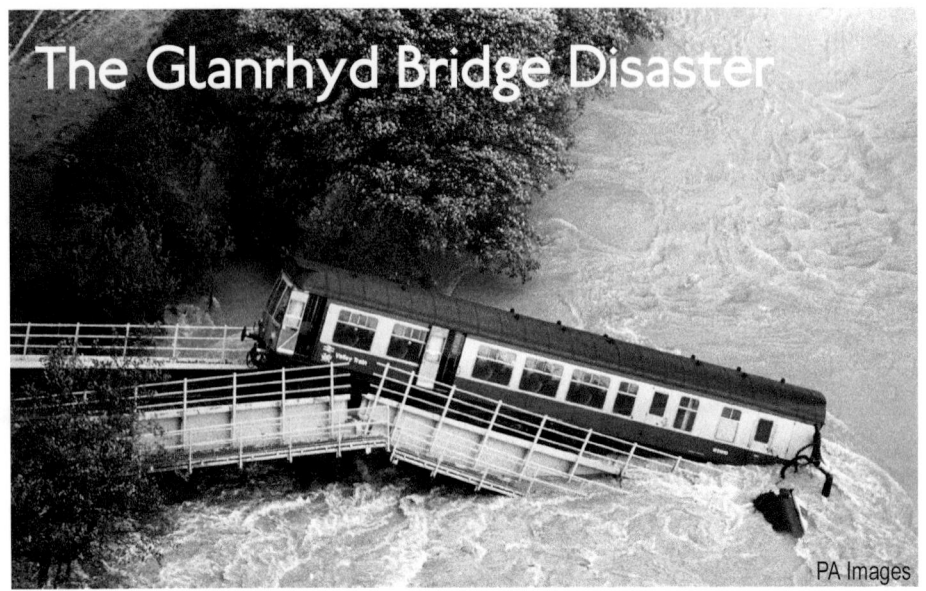
PA Images

Tragedy struck the line in the great storm of 1987, when the Glanrhyd bridge between Llandovery and Llandeilo collapsed, with the loss of four lives.

The early Swansea to Shrewsbury service had ten passengers on board, including several British Rail staff who were accompanying the train to inspect the route after reports of flooding and track damage had been received the previous day. Glanrhyd bridge had been partially washed away overnight in the swollen river after what is remembered as biblical quantities of rain had fallen. The driver was unaware of the situation, and the train plunged into the raging River Towy.

The rear carriage remained on what was left of the bridge, however the front carriage was submerged in the floodwaters where the coupling held it in place for a while until the force of the water sheared the coupling and it was washed away. Rescuers had not been able to access the carriage, in which four of the ten passengers drowned - driver Mr J M Churchill, an elderly married couple, Mr and Mrs W B Evans, and Simon Penny, a teenage schoolboy.

Following the disaster, more robust safety measures were put in place. Network Rail has teams of divers carrying out regular underwater examinations of all rail over river bridges.
When a flood warning is issued, further assessments are undertaken with remote monitoring equipment and visual inspections.

A poem written by Thomas Corbett, (a postman from Llanfihangel Rhydithon) about the journey of the first locomotive to run between Knucklas Station and Penybont Junction under the direction of Mr George Moreton (Chief Engineer) in October 1864.

They started from Knucklas o'er a viaduct grand,
Where the scenes of the Teme are at your command;
In the month of October, in the year of sixty-four,
An engine they started which ne'er ran before.

The engine they started, 'twas late in the night,
When the peasantry around did sadly affright;
The sound of the whistle so loudly did call,
Through the central valley, by cottage and hall.

Near to Llancoch, where the tunnel does run,
The jolly old huntsman did fire a gun;
In passing Pyecorner, the young master did stare,
And declared, the engine ran faster than Fille de L'air.

In passing Llangunllo, the bells did they ring,
Michael from Cork danced and Biddy did sing
In the midst of their joy, poor Biddy did faint,
When Mac cried 'Och murther - there lies a dead saint'!

As they passed by Lea Hall, Creig and the old gravel-pit
Where poor Vulcan the Blacksmith fell down in a fit;
In passing the Maylord and tamed Cwm-y-Gaist
The whistle it sounded - a long loud shrill blast.

Onwards for Lusson near the Central Railway,
Ally called Billy and bade him to pray;
Then Billy fell down, and his mother did say
"The old Nick is coming right up the railway"

In passing the Dollys, they sounded a call
Which echoed aloud through the woods of Old Hall,
They passed Red Lean and the farms of Teedee,
The old lady called N.G. the wonder to see

Old Francis the butcher, who was laid in his bed,
Declared he had heard a call from the dead.
Then onward to Dolyjenkin where the engine did stop
And Moreton regaled with brandy-and-gin hot.

Reflections on Dolau Station at around Eight o'clock on an evening in June

Now golden sunlight cuts the landscape keen;
The rushing swallows round me twittering fly;
A curlew bubbles in his field nearby.
Gaunt cypress trees - a line of deep green -
Divide the living from the dead unseen.
Profusely lupins' coloured spires point high
To challenge formal beds that nearby lie
In well marked lines, and ordered peace serene.
A blasting horn breaks through the clear, soft air;
The train approaches down the distant straight;
Its ageing coaches slow their rumbling pace:
Then warning lights flash on and claxons blare.
The clanking train slows down but does not wait;
And soon warm silence softly claims her place.

Kevin Kell

A journey along the line

In this guide to the route, the railway terminology of "up" and "down" lines are used - Up denotes the direction of travel towards Shrewsbury (on the left as you travel to Shrewsbury), Down denotes travel in the direction of Swansea.

Shrewsbury is a bustling historic town that is well worth exploring. Attractions include medieval side streets, numerous historic buildings, the Quarry garden near the river Severn and a military museum in the castle, adjacent to the station.

Interior, Severn Bridge Junction signal Box. Network Rail

Trains leave for Swansea from the imposing station once known as Shrewsbury General, distinguishing it from the town's (now closed) Abbey, Abbey Foregate, and West stations. For the first 20 miles, the route follows the main Manchester to Cardiff line, before diverging at Craven Arms. As we head out of Shrewsbury you can't miss the impressive sight of Severn Bridge Junction signal box, the largest remaining manual signal box in the world, with 180 levers.

At Sutton Bridge Junction the trackbed on the down side was the start of the Severn Valley route, through Ironbridge and Bridgnorth to Kidderminster. The Severn Valley Railway, one of Britain's premier heritage lines, now operates between Bridgnorth and Kidderminster.

> **"**My father was the guard on the last train from Swansea Victoria to Shrewsbury. For some years I travelled with my father helping with his duties e.g. counting passengers, recording arrival and departure times, checking the pigeons and livestock etc.**"**
>
> *Jean Johnson*

On the up side, the line to Aberystwyth and the Cambrian Coast heads west. The hills of the Welsh borderland rise on both sides of the main line - The Long Mynd, Wenlock Edge and Caer Caradoc. The section south from Shrewsbury was opened in 1853 and was worked jointly by the L&NW and Great Western Railways.

29

Church Stretton is the first station, serving a pleasant 18th century town, which is a popular destination for walkers. You may notice the plaque on the platform concerning the town's longitude relative to Greenwich and hence its difference in 'real time' from GMT.

Just beyond the station we reach the top of our first climb into the hills and as we descend towards Craven Arms, look out for the embankment just visible on the up side. This was Stretford Bridge Junction, where the famously eccentric Bishop's Castle Railway joined the main line, until its closure in 1935. The line was financially disastrous and spent 69 of its 72 years in receivership.

At Craven Arms Crossing signal box the driver will receive the single line token for the section to Knighton. This is an essential element of the signalling system and ensures that only one train can be in the relevant section at any time. At the rest of the passing loops the driver will operate the token instruments himself in a hut on the platform, having received permission to do so from the signalman by telephone: this system enables the Pantyffynnon signalman to supervise operations over the 79 miles between his box and Craven Arms.

The train now crosses to the up main line. calls at the station and just beyond the platform turns onto the Heart of Wales Line proper, encountering a sharp 90° curve after which the route heads for the Welsh border in a south westerly direction.

Bucknell Station

You should catch a glimpse of Stokesay Castle arguably England's finest fortified manor house, on the left as the train heads round the curve.
Craven Arms was a busy market town and centre for agriculture, with large numbers of livestock arriving here for transport by rail. Today it still hosts a market, along with the Shropshire Hills Discovery Centre and Land of Lost Content (The National Museum of Popular British Culture).

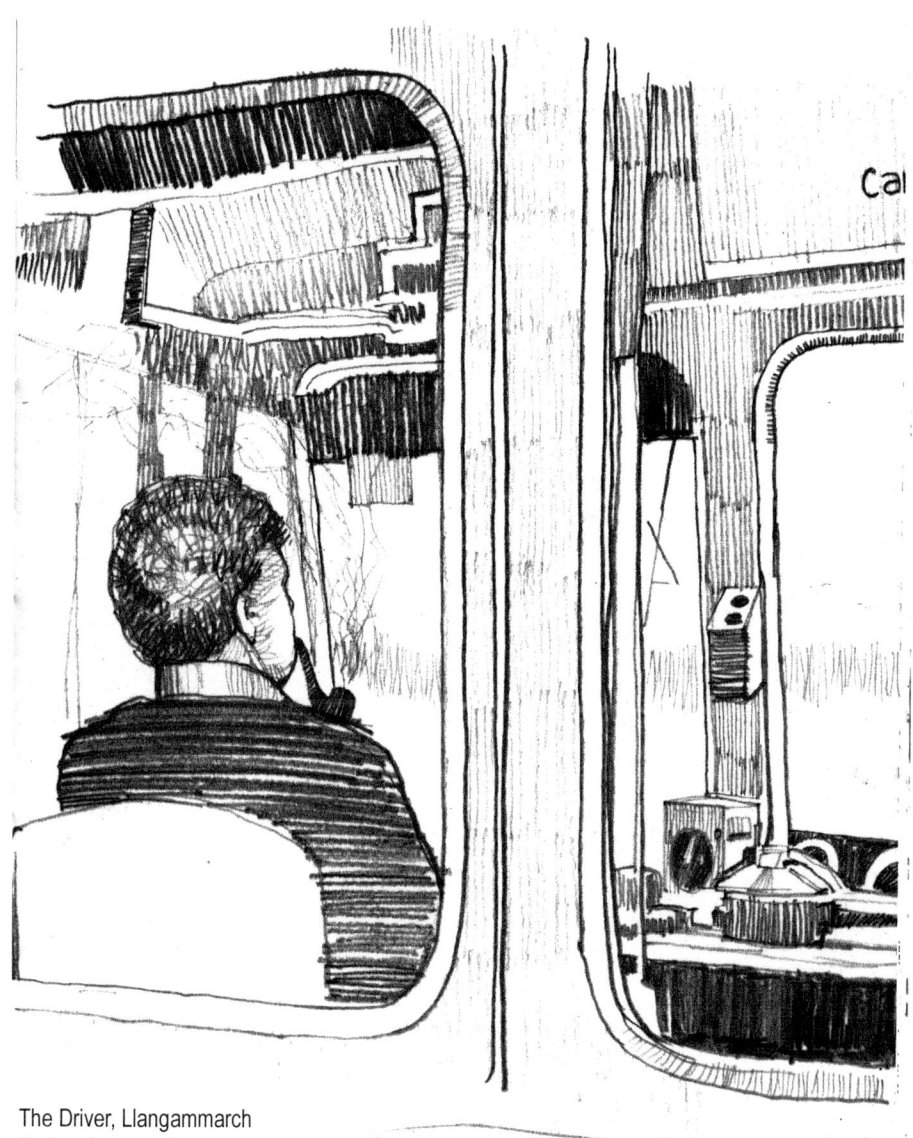

The Driver, Llangammarch
Dorian Spencer Davies

Our first request stop is Broome, Shropshire's least used station, where the station building was demolished in the 1960's, but the goods shed survives in private hands. Next the line crosses the river Clun,
Approaching Knucklas Viaduct, Geoff Charles, 1983 NLW

which links Clungunford - said by a well-known old Shropshire rhyme to be one of the four "prettiest villages under the sun" - with the other three - Clunton, Clunbury and Clun.

Our next station is Hopton Heath, with its staggered platforms, now only the down platform is in use. The former station house is privately owned, and the weighbridge building also survives.

Heading down a long straight we can see Bedstone school, with the Clun forest in the distance.

Bucknell is a small village clustered around the river Redlake. The attractive station building is now a private house. It has the first of several ungated level crossings with only traffic lights warning road vehicles and a white flashing light to tell the train driver if the traffic lights are working. At certain farm crossings, where visibility is poor and which lack telephones for contact with the signalman, severe speed restrictions are imposed in the interests of safety.

Just before the station, on the down side you may catch a glimpse of the Jolly's Circus yard - the old station yard, where the goods shed and weighbridge building still exist. At the time of writing this is up for sale. Behind the circus yard is Davies timber yard, established in 1860, three years before the railway arrived. The business is still owned by the same family today.

As we head to Knighton, the river Teme meanders alongside the line, along with the English-Welsh border. Knighton, on the River Teme, is an interesting place with the station just in England but the town itself in Wales. The border runs through the station car park!

The Welsh name for Knighton is Tref-y-Clawdd, meaning 'town on the dyke', which refers to the rampart built by King Offa of Mercia over a thousand years ago along the Welsh marches. The bustling town is well worth visiting, with many independent shops, The Offa's Dyke Centre and the Norman Bryn y Castell behind the Community Centre

Back at the station, the passing loop was reinstated in 1990 to break up the excessively long single line section between Craven Arms and Llandrindod (until 1964 the Craven Arms to Knighton and Llanbister Road to Llandrindod sections were double track). The first of the small grey sheds where the drivers exchange tokens along the line can be seen. The impressive station building was once the headquarters of the Knighton Railway, and is currently awaiting a new tenant, having formerly been a veterinary practice. Some of the original station buildings still exist in the yard, now occupied by Teme Valley Tractors.

Having crossed the border just south of Knighton, the line begins to climb away from the Teme to Knucklas (Cnwclas) station, then across the 13 arch Grade II Listed viaduct. Some of the stone for this impressive structure is said to have come from Knucklas castle, built by the Mortimers in about 1220-25 on the hill on the southern side of the village. The train is now climbing at 1 in 60, clinging to the hillside past Heyope Church in the valley below.

Llangunllo Station 1900 - 1910 P.B.Abery NLW

As we continue south, the Spaceguard Centre is visible on the down side, with its telescope domes and planetarium. It is open to the public and well worth a visit.

Llangynllo tunnel (647 yards long) brings us to the summit of the line at 980 feet above sea level, making this the highest operational standard gauge railway in Wales.

Again, Llangynllo station is reduced to a wooden station shelter, whilst the former station building is a private house. Note the bay window overlooking the line - formerly a very unusual signal box! At present the station is almost invisible from the road, its access is between the two private houses in the former station yard.

As we round a right hand curve the village of Llangynllo can be seen over a mile away on the down side in the valley. Maylord Hill is awash with a sea of bluebells for the benefit of those travelling in the late spring.

Soon we arrive at Llanbister Road, a railway euphemism that means the station is a significant distance from the settlement it claims to serve. Contemporary railways use the term "parkway" in the same manner. In the case of Llanbister Road, it came about because of the need to space signal boxes out at reasonably even distances, and this was the point at which the line changed from single to double track. The few properties that surround the station were all originally railway workers' accommodation.

Moving onwards, the line descends into the valley of the River Aran to Dolau, where the splendid gardens have received numerous awards for the local community volunteers who look after the station. The small waiting room has a collection of photos, poetry and reminiscences of the line in its heyday.

The railway handcart on the platform is a relic of the Elan Valley Railway - a standard gauge line built especially for the construction of the Elan Valley dams, some miles to the west. The line was dismantled after construction finished and few traces remain.

Dolau Station waiting room

After a couple of miles the train passes through the Pen-y-Bont tunnel (404 yards long) to reach Pen-y-Bont station, with its ex LMS station name boards.

Near here an extension to the Kington railway was once planned to cross our line on its way to Aberystwyth. Its promoters would have struggled to find a suitable route around the slopes of the Radnor Forest (2000 feet above sea level), which can be seen just before entering the tunnel.

The line passes the village of Crossgates, bridges the River lthon twice, then a level crossing greets us on the outskirts of Llandrindod Wells. This is the administrative and commercial centre for Powys with a population of 5000. The station has a passing loop and its station building houses an independent ticket office with many years of railway ticketing experience, runs a very busy counter and mail order service.

The signal box was moved in 1990 from the level crossing to its present site, where it was used as a museum. However with the passing of the curator it is now destined for a home on a heritage railway.

Under the station canopy (not the original, this graced the front of Powys Council offices until 1990) a stone marks the spot where, in 1952, Queen Elizabeth II first set foot in Wales. She arrived by Royal Train to open the Claerwen Reservoir in the Elan Valley 15 miles to the west.

Queen Victoria arrives at Llandrindod Wells

A plaque on Llandridod Wells station bench in memoriam of the late Tom Clift. (1954 - 2012). A lifelong railwayman who was a senior manager at Arriva Trains, as well as other railway companies. He wrote a well regarded book on the line in 1982

Llandrindod has wide Edwardian streets, several grand Victorian hotels and plenty of large elegant Victorian shops and houses, a reminder of its past glory as Wales's leading spa town. In its heyday, the town's rail services included through carriages from London, with up to 100,000 visitors arriving by train each season. There is an annual Victorian Festival, which is well worth a visit, and includes "Queen Victoria" arriving by train - on an Arriva class 153!

Approaching Builth Road you will see the original goods shed and railway cottages on the up side. Immediately after the station the line passes over the trackbed of the Mid Wales Railway from Moat Lane (near Newtown) to Brecon, which was closed in 1962.

The former low level station building can be seen below on the down side, and is now a private residence after spending many years as The Cambrian Arms. The two stations were connected with a path and a water-powered goods lift.
The original station was called Llechryd when opened by the Mid Wales Railway, and became Builth Road in 1889.

The station building is now divided into flats, and some of the residents maintain the gardens on the platform. You may sometimes see the resident (but unofficial) station cat.

Driver obtaining the token in the hut at Llandovery

36

EUSTON EXPRESS AT LLANDRINDOD WELLS STATION
(L.&N.W.RAILWAY)

Builth Wells is a pleasant market town about 2 miles away down the valley, and the Royal Welsh Agricultural Society's showground is just outside the town. Special services from Cardiff combined with a shuttle bus and reduced entry fees ensure packed trains each July for the Annual Royal Welsh Show.

A timber yard now occupies the lower yard where the loop once joined the LNWR to the Mid Wales Railway. This curve was mainly used for goods traffic, and no trace is visible.

Our train now crosses the Wye and climbs through the short Rhosferig (64 yards long) and Cilmeri (115 yards) tunnels to Cilmeri station in the lrfon Valley. On the hill above the line on the up side is a monument to Llywelyn the Last, Prince of Wales, who was killed here by the English in 1282.

At Garth you can see the remains of a cattle dock siding at the southern end of the platform, behind this was a small goods yard (now housing). Next we reach Llangammarch. This is another of the spas of Mid Wales which, along with Llandrindod, Builth and Llanwrtyd was well publicised by the L&NWR and its successor the London Midland & Scottish.

The station boasted a small goods yard, where bottled spa water was despatched, the town's barium water being the only local spa water suitable for bottling.

Llanwrtyd itself has a passing loop and serves a village of about 500 people. Following the discovery in 1732 by the Rev. Theophilus Evans of waters claimed to have healing properties, Llanwrtyd Wells became a spa town, with the sulphurous waters referred to as Ffynnon Ddrewllyd "Stinking Well" because of the smell of hydrogen sulphide. The LLanwrtyd & District Heritage & Arts Centre have an excellent display of the town's history.

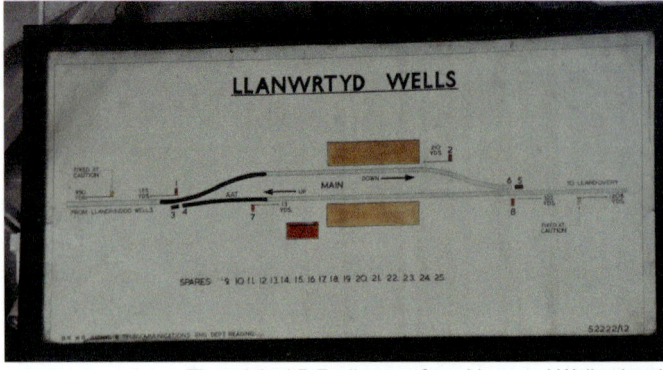

The original B.R. diagram from Llanwrtyd Wells signal box. Now in the Gwilli Railway Museum

Local sporting activities take on an eccentric nature here, with the town hosting the annual 'World Alternative Games'. So if you fancy your skill at bog snorkelling, worm charming or slow cycling this delightful town is the place to be every August! The up side station building survives, and has recently become the office of the Heart of Wales Line Development Company. An information board gives details and photographs of the station's history. A grating, also on the up side of the line is all that remains of the water crane - essential infrastructure at many stations in the days of steam.

The scenery becomes more mountainous as the train climbs at 1 in 70 to Sugar Loaf Summit (820 ft above sea level), where the tiny platforms, which formerly served the railway cottages, situated above the cutting can still be seen. The station is another request stop, and has the dubious distinction of being the least used station in Wales, with only 132 passengers in 2017. It closed altogether in 1965, but reopened in 1984, originally just on summer Sundays, but is now a full time request stop for all services.

The over bridge immediately after the station has an unusual feature, with a small riveted iron aqueduct attached, containing a fast flowing stream.
(see photo above).

The narrow portal of the Sugar Loaf tunnel greets us on our way over the summit. The 1000 yard tunnel marks the boundaries of Powys and Carmarthenshire, and the watersheds of the rivers Wye and Towy.

There have been several instances where geological issues have caused closure: in 1926 there was a landslip at the northern end, and in 1949 the tunnel was closed for two months following a partial collapse of the lining. In 1991 the tunnel was treated with a pioneering spray on concrete lining as a result of bulges in the aging brickwork.

Above: The southbound train stops just before Llandovery Station, so that the driver can pull a handle to operate the level crossing before proceeding.

Below: Engineering works, Llandovery, 1986
Anthony Birdwood

As we leave the tunnel, the line perches on a ledge on the hillside, descending at 1 in 60, with a magnificent view to the south across the Vale of Towy (Towy). As the line curves left the magnificent Cynghordy viaduct can be glimpsed.

The structure is an impressive 18 arch curved stone construction, 283 yards long, and towers 102 feet above the Afon Bran.
Cynghordy station is busier than might be expected - as with so many other villages on the line, remoteness rules out a daily bus service. The village still boasts a school, but has lost the brickworks, which provided bricks for construction of the railway.

Llandovery is a typical Welsh market town, with a small public school (Llandovery College) and the remains of a castle. The station has a passing loop but there is little evidence of its former importance - there were two engine sheds, a goods yard, turntable and a controller's office in addition to 3 delivery vehicles and over 50 staff at one point. Banking engines were stationed here to give assistance to heavy freight trains tackling the climb to Sugar Loaf summit. The station building was refurbished with the aid of EU grants, the café was opened as a community enterprise in 2010 and has a small library of books and photos about the line. It also hosts regular poetry evenings and displays by local artists. The town is well worth a look for its numerous crafts, antiques and charity shops.

From here to Llandeilo the route was owned jointly by the LMS and GWR and the train follows the Towy through Llanwrda, with its ungated level crossing and staggered platforms on to Llangadog, where there was a large creamery that had a rail connection until the 1970's. The creamery itself closed in 2005 and a pet food factory now occupies the site.

About a mile further on, at Glanrhyd, we cross the Towy on a substantial girder bridge, built to replace the original bridge that collapsed during extreme flooding in October 1987.

The line continues on a 1 in 100 descent past the site of two stations both closed in 1955. Glanrhyd is visible on the up side, the station house (now a private dwelling) and platform are located just after an ungated level crossing.

> "After finishing school early in the 2nd war and being stationed around Birmingham, I still continued to use the line, but now from Shrewsbury to Llangammarch. I used ot leave Birmingham about 9pm on the London to Birkenhead train, stop over generally in the WMCA in Shrewsbury and await the Milk and Mail Swansea train, arriving in Llangammarch about 7am.
>
> From the station platform of Llangammarch one could look up to the Myndd Eppynt and see the scar where a Wellington bomber crashed "
>
> Denzil Jones

40

Above: Collecting the token, Pantyffynnon. Geoff Charles, 1983 NLW

Below: An unidentified Black 5 near Pontardulais, June 1963

G.W.R. Collet pannier tank 3796 at Llandybie, June 1963

The former Talley Road station, also on the up side, is named after the village six miles away rather than the somewhat closer Manordeilo.

Until 1963 Llandeilo was the junction for Carmarthen, the branch curved west just beyond the Towy bridge south of the station. There is an elegant pedestrian suspension bridge over the river on the down side of the station and the Llandeilo station hub can be seen in the station yard.

Llandeilo is named after one of the better-known Welsh saints, Saint Teilo. The early Christian settlement that developed around the Saint Teilo's Church prospered and by the early 9th century it had attained considerable ecclesiastical status as the seat of a Bishop-Abbot. The Church of St Teilo soon became a 'mother church' to the surrounding district, acquiring an extensive estate and possessing one of Wales' most beautiful and finely illustrated manuscripts - the Gospel Book of Saint Teilo. This was moved to Lichfield Cathedral in the 9th century, where it became commonly known as the Lichfield Gospels

Today Llandeilo is a busy town, with many independent shops, and a reputation for local arts and crafts. It also hosts several festivals and was named one of the best places to live in Wales in 2017.

Leaving Llandeilo we pass over the last bridge over the river Towy, a rare example of an early lattice truss bridge.

Original GWR interlocking gate mechanism, Pantyffynnon level crossing

The former Llandybie signal box still operating at Bronwydd Arms. Gwilli Railway.

Dinefwr Castle is situated on a hill to the west. This imposing ruin stands 250 feet above the river and was the seat of Rhys ap Gruffydd, one of the early kings of Wales, though is sadly only visible from the road, not the train.

Less than a mile from Llandeilo we arrive in Ffairfach. Now limited to a half barrier level crossing and single platform, it once boasted a signal box (now in use on the heritage Gwilli Railway as a museum) and private sidings for the gasworks and Co-op creamery, in use until the 1960's.

The line now climbs at 1 in 105 on sharp curves over the 1857 extension of the original Llanelly Railway. A couple of miles after Ffairfach the site of Derwydd Road station can be seen on the down side, where some disused coal staithes survive.

The former Ffairfach signal box, now the Gwilli Railway Museum

Above: Ammanford signal box, May 1986 *Jon Critchley*
Below: Ammanford, 37227 and an unidentified Class 37, May 1986 *Jon Critchley*

44

Two car DMU at Pantyffynnon, May 1986 *Jon Critchley*

On the upside beyond Cilyrychen level crossing we can see the quarries, which used to be connected to the main line by a siding known as the 'Limestone Branch'. The large structures set into the side of the quarry are lime kilns, designed by RK Penson, a leading Gothic Revival architect and the brother of the Shrewsbury station architect TK Penson. These were once the largest limestone quarries in Europe, by 1900 there were nine kilns, 50 feet high and capable of producing 20 tons of lime per day. Lime burning ended at the site in 1973.

Llandybie, where the station is looked after the local primary school, is another stations whose signal box has gained a new lease of life at the heritage Gwilli Railway. The current station has a single platform and shelter, but used to serve the lime quarries and a colliery, with a staff of 20 until the 1950's.

The former mining town of Ammanford is the largest on the line excluding the termini. The station was formerly named Tirydail to distinguish it from the 'other' Ammanford station on the GWR branch from Brynamman (which we join at Pantyffnon). The Llandeilo to Pontarddulais section was actually owned by the GWR, but the LNWR/LMS exercised "running powers" over it to reach Swansea.

Leaving Ammanford the line passes the leisure centre on the down side followed by a road overbridge. Immediately after the bridge is the site of the short lived Parcyrhun Halt, opened in 1936 and closed in 1955. Opposite the halt was a network of lines to various collieries. A disused rail bridge can be glimpsed in the trees on the up side.

As we pass over the level crossing into Pantyffynnon station you may well see the crossing keeper, this being one of the last manually operated crossings in Wales. The station had a small but busy freight yard, with an engine shed and turntable, and was the junction for the branch to Brynammen. The primary freight traffic consisted of tinplate and coal, with coal trains departing for Swansea Docks and elsewhere, but this traffic is now greatly reduced. It stopped altogether in 1988, but single loco working to Twairgaith resumed in 2009 with coal traffic from the open cast mine. Network Rail restored the elegant station building in 2017.

The train arrives at Llanwrtyd Wells
Dorian Spencer Davies

The former Llandybie signal box, now operating at The Gwilli Railway

At the 1892 GWR signal box, our driver hands over the single line token for the last time. From here our journey is controlled from the modern box at Port Talbot, about 22 miles away by rail.

Although the scenery is now less striking, the line, formerly double track, is still of great interest. Pontarddulais had a small marshalling yard and four platforms, serving several tinplate works and being the junction for Grovesend colliery and for the LNWR main line to Swansea Victoria, which was closed in 1964. For six years trains terminated at Llanelli, until common sense prevailed and services were extended to Swansea. All trains now bear right on the GWR route and pass through the short and narrow Hendy tunnel (88 yards long).

The Loughor estuary is now visible on the down side of the line, and the northerly part of the Gower Peninsula comes into view. As the line becomes double track once again, we reach Llangennech station, situated beside the estuary mudflats, a haven for wading birds. The estuary also supports a small cockle industry. Once again, Llangennech was a much busier station in its heyday, with a spur to the tinplate works, collieries and a Naval depot.

Continuing past the Loughor estuary, which is at points within a few yards of the line, the Huntsman chemical works is visible on the down side, before we curve inland and reach Bynea station. This is followed by the Trostre steelworks on the upside, a large tinplate manufacturing centre and steel recycling centre. Scrubland separates the old and new stretches of the HOWL as it joins the South Wales main line.

> "Craven Arms was very busy. This chap, Garnie Gwitham his name was, he was a clerk in the goods shed at Craven Arms. Apart from that there were three clerks and a chief clerk in the goods shed itself and then there were a couple of three others that did the manual work or whatever was in. A chap used to go out with a great big horse and dray delivering round Craven Arms because there wasn't lorries and motors in those days. There was two shunters, a foreman shunter and one under him in the yard and they worked three shifts. You'd be shunting all different wagons and forming trains, pushing coal, timber and sugar beet".
>
> P Lloyd

The official '0' miles marker stands before a very battered sign marking Llandeilo Junction, 223 miles from Paddington. This line was originally a GWR broad gauge line, being converted to standard gauge in 1872.

Less than half a mile from the steelworks we reach Llanelli station where Heart of Wales Trains reverse for the last stage of their journey to Swansea. Llanelli is a busy town with a large shopping centre, and is a focal point for the valleys to the north. The town was formerly a prosperous manufacturing centre, with coal, tinplate copper and pottery manufacture based here. In the 1890's, South Wales produced 80% of the world's tinplate. The first canned beer in the UK was produced here by the Felinfoel brewery in 1935, using tinplate from the Trostre steelworks.

Continuing along the main line, we pass the site of Loughor station, closed in 1960, and cross the Loughor estuary on a new viaduct constructed in

An excellent collection of old signs from the line are preserved in the Kidderminster station museum at the Severn Valley Railway. Well worth a visit. www.svr.co.uk

2013. Next to the line we can see a section of the old viaduct has been preserved. This imposing wooden structure was the last remaining wooden viaduct built by Brunel.

At Gowerton the abutments of the former direct route of the Central Wales Line into Swansea Victoria are visible just to the west of the station. The train now climbs steeply at 1 in 50 past Llaunarluydd to Cockett where the closed platforms can still be seen just before we enter the 788 yard Cockett tunnel. This structure caused Brunel serious difficulties due to the soft and unstable ground, several supporting buttresses can be seen overhead on the Swansea side of the tunnel, supporting the cutting walls.

From the summit here we descend sharply to Landore, where the train maintenance depot is situated amidst a triangle of lines. We join the main line from London and Cardiff at Swansea Loop West Junction and our train terminates at Swansea, where the station was known as "High Street" to distinguish it from the LMS termini at Victoria and St. Thomas.

Swansea (Abertawe) has a lot to offer the visitor. It was the home of the first passenger railway in the world, the Swansea and Mumbles, whose services (initially horse drawn) began in 1807 and ended in 1960. There are numerous shops, a University College, Museums and an Art Gallery. The Gower Peninsula was the first place to be officially designated an Area of Outstanding Natural Beauty in 1956 and is easily accessible by bus from the city centre. Part of the old docks area has been converted into a yachting marina, and in 1992 the River Tawe barrage was completed, creating a lake stretching upstream towards Morriston. There is a summer ferry service to Cork in the Irish Republic.

The Heart of Wales Line has survived various attempts at closure, and a journey along it remains a unique and delightful railway experience - long may it continue!

RADNORSHIRE

LLANDRINDOD WELLS

● THE TOURIST CENTRE OF WALES

The Ideal Centre for Tourists, etc.
Britain's Best Bowling Greens :: Golf :: Tennis :: Boating :: Fishing
Swimming Pool :: Orchestra :: Dancing :: Concerts

Free Illustrated Guide (Postage 4d.) from David Williams, Information Bureau (Dept. H.G.)

Knighton Station 2018. The goods shed is behind the trees, now in use as part of the tractor workshop. The two timber sheds are still in use, though in poor condition. The attic room above the new platform shelter was the former Knighton Railway boardroom.

Knighton Station, Ordnance Survey 1:2500 1928 edition shows the extent of the railway yard and sidings

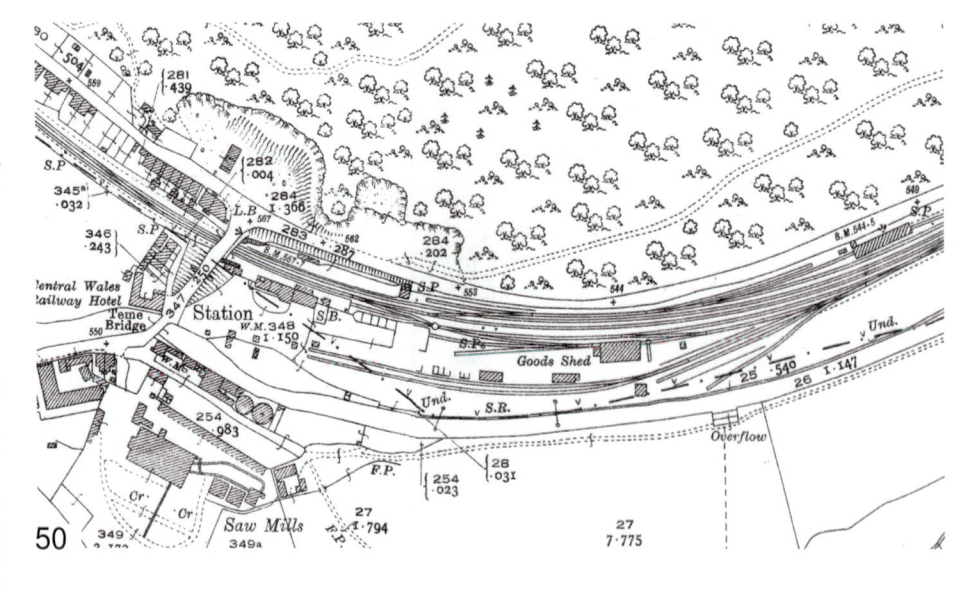

The Railway Today

At the time of writing the line continues to provide an essential service to the small communities in rural Mid Wales. There are however, serious limitations to the usability of the line for many people when some services have a gap of over four hours between them. Certainly timings have improved over previous service levels, with commuting by rail now being a practical option for some.

After a year of celebration and events marking the 150th anniversary there was further cause for celebration as the new franchise for Wales and Borders announced improvements in services along the line. Although not everything that pressure groups have been asking for has been delivered, there is promise of a big improvement.

However the reliability of the 153 units currently used on the line does negate that somewhat. A recent incident with the failure of a 153 as it arrived in Swansea in the early afternoon led to taxis being arranged for the next return service, and passengers for later services left waiting for replacement buses with little or no information as to their arrival times.

This is not a state of affairs that will help improve passenger numbers, and illustrates that the new franchise holder needs to not only deliver the promised improvment of refurbished rolling stock, but have enough units in depot in case of breakdowns, as was the case in the days of British Rail.

44871 leads 45407 "The Lancashire Fusilier" across Cynghordy Viaduct with the Cardiff - Preston leg of the "Great Britain VI" railtour.April 22, 2013.   *Stephen Thomas*

TFW have indicated that there will be new trains for the line by 2022, and recently hinted that there could possibly be more standby stock on depot in the future. However, in these days of privatisation, the availability of suitable rolling stock in the UK is somewhat limited.

Tickets and passes:

With limited ticket purchasing facilities on the route most tickets are bought on the train from the guard. There are a number of options for discounted travel, in addition to the usual railcards that are available. The independent ticket office at Llandrindod Wells is able to issue all manner of tickets and passes for UK rail travel as well as on the line itself.

Heart of Wales Line Railcard:

The railcard is available to residents aged 16 or over in specific postcodes along the route, and to HOWLTA members. It costs £10 per year and gives 1/3rd discount on rail fares for the line. It can be purchased at Swansea, Llanelli, Llandrindod and Shrewsbury ticket offices.

Rover tickets are also available, with The Heart of Wales Circular Two Day Ranger offering great value for money. It gives a circular route with unlimited travel in either direction. They can be bought from any railway station ticket office or on board the train.

Concessionary fares:

All holders of Welsh bus passes can travel free between 1st October and 31st March along the line between Swansea and Shrewsbury. This scheme is available to all holders of a Concessionary Travel Pass issued by any Welsh Local Authority.

> "One event in the line what was great importance was the Railwayman's Show held every year at Llanwrtyd Wells. The show was held at the Abernant Lake and it was a day out for the Railwaymen. It was a combined show of G.W.R. and L.N.W.R. (Later L.M.S.). Men from the south, Swansea, Llanelli, meeting men from the north, Shrewsbury, Craven Arms, clerks, signalmen, shunters, guards, all the different railway grades meeting. Railwaymen on the Mid Wales line were always keen gardeners. No trains ran on Good Friday and that was the day that gardens were dug etc".
>
> C. Boyd.

A Brighter Future?

There is no doubt that the consistent campaigning by HOWLTA and others has paid off, with continued investment and development of the line and some improvements to services. The line has an unparalleled level of support through the association, the station adoption groups and the development company. These groups have been successful in raising funds and obtaining grants for station improvements and developments, and the successful adoption of stations by various schools helps to foster community interest at an early age.

However, at the end of the day people will only use the service if it's easy and practical for them to do so, and the line does need to appeal to locals as well at the vital tourism trade.

Realistically, the current level of service - four trains per day each way with early morning short working at each end of the line - needs to improve to give a frequency of at least one train every two hours, ideally with some through services to Crewe and Cardiff. These improvements also need to extend to Sundays, for the benefit the leisure and tourism sectors. The current Sunday service level of two trains per day isi very limiting for the leisure and tourist traffic, which is vital for the numerous tourism based businesses in this area of Wales.

Knighton goods shed, now in use as part of a tractor workshop

Station usage statistics.

Station	2016-17 Entries & Exits
Broome	782
Hopton Heath	1,332
Bucknell	5516
Knighton	20,714
Knucklas	3,670
Llyngunllo	720
Llanbister Road	860
Dolau	1,528
Pen-y-bont	1,858
Llandrindod Wells	40,768
Builth Road	7,672
Cilmeri	1,698
Garth	974
Llangammarch	1,996
Llanwrtyd Wells	7,484
Sugar Loaf	228
Cynghordy	994
Llandovery	15,596
Llanwrda	2,206
Llangadog	5,324
Llandeilo	18,764
Ffairfach	2,552
Llandybie	9,382
Ammanford	19,428
Pantyffynnon	4,076
Pontarddulais	5,522
Llangennech	3,064
Bynea	1,930
Total	186,638

Only stations that are solely on the Heart of Wales Line are included here.

Others, such as Craven Arms and Llanelli, have numerous other services stopping there.

The line has the dubious distinction of having both the least used station in Wales (Sugar Loaf) and the least used station in Shropshire (Broome).

Though arguably it has some of the most charming and memorable as well.

Although the overall picture shows a steady number of passengers using the line, Sugar Loaf had a surprising increase in numbers by 72%, up from 132 passengers in 2015-16.

Figures provided by Welsh Government statistics office: https://statswales.gov.wales

More than numbers

The least used station in Wales has a visitors book. It's in a plastic box under the shelter. Here are some of this year's comments.

If we measured the benefit to society of such stations in purely economic terms it would have closed long ago. Thankfully, the wider British public have more of an attachment to their railways than many bean counters, so we have managed to hold onto some of the delights of our rail network like Sugar Loaf Station.

> We got engaged here today !.!.8
> # make your intent clear
> # all the stations

> Great views
> 30th Wedding Anniversary
> Worth the visit. So quiet

> we came and remembered my sister who liked this place

> NO TRAINS · BUT A LOVELY PLACE.

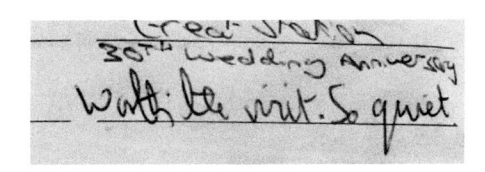

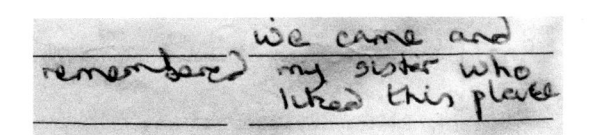

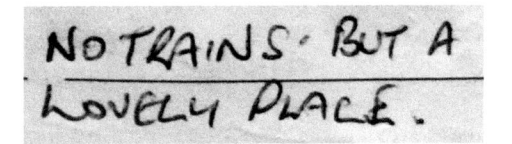

Transport for Wales

At the time of writing, the new 15-year franchise for Wales and Border rail services has just been awarded to Keolis Amey (KA) who have taken over from Arriva. The contract is being operated under the banner of "Transport for Wales" on a non-profit basis as an "Operator and Development Partner" rather than a traditional Train Operating Company (TOC).

Considerable improvements to infrastructure and services have been promised for the whole of Wales; those affecting the Heart of Wales Line include extra services and upgrading of stations and ticketing facilities.

Timetable improvements:

By December 2022

Monday to Friday: 5 trains per day along the length of the line in each direction, plus a short working between Llandrindod and Crewe, and a short working between Llandovery and Swansea.

Saturday: 5 trains per day along the length of the line in each direction.

Sunday: 2 trains per day along the full length of the line in each direction.

By May 2023

Mon to Fri: 5 trains per day along the full length of the line in each direction, plus 2 short workings between Llandrindod and Shrewsbury, and 2 short workings between Llandovery and Swansea. One of the Llandrindod to Shrewsbury workings will be extended to/from Crewe each day, morning and evening. The evening short working to Llandovery will be extended to start at Cardiff from May 2019.

Saturdays: 5 trains per day along the full length of the line in each direction, plus 1 short working between Llandrindod and Shrewsbury, and 1 short working between Llandovery and Swansea.

Sundays: 2 trains per day along the full length of the line in each direction, plus 1 short working between Llandrindod and Shrewsbury, and 1 short working between Llandovery and Swansea.

TRAFNIDIAETH CYMRU
TRANSPORT FOR WALES

Rolling stock:

From 2022 refurbished Class 170 "Turbostar" 2-car diesel multiple units will operate on the line, with information screens, PRM toilets, air conditioning, wifi and power sockets. In the interim, additional single-car units will be added for the extra services.

Tickets:

The existing senior citizens' bus pass concession between October and March will continue long term. In addition, the Heart of Wales Line Railcard is now a contractual requirement with the new franchise, and free travel for under 5s will be extended to under 11s, and half-price fares extended to 16-18 year olds. Additionally, under 16s will travel free off peak.

All stations will have ticket machines by April 2022, with new technology such as contactless payment.

Stations:

Ongoing cleaning and "enhancement" programme for all stations, with new or refurbished platform shelters. In addition, wifi will be available on all stations by December 2020, and cycle storage and monitored CCTV will be installed on all stations by March 2023.

> The railway was like one big family. It was handed down from father to son, great tradition that you could be on the railway. There were very few buses. It didn't matter where anybody wanted to go it was always on the railways. It was quite an attraction you know. People made a habit, especially at Knighton, they'd make a habit of going to the station at half past seven in the evening to see the last train come in. Always curiosity to see who came.
> *T Powell*

The Heart of Wales Line Development Company

The Heart of Wales Line Development Company (DevCo) was founded with the objective of promoting and developing the Heart of Wales Line to benefit local people, businesses and visitors. It is part of Community Rail Wales, and supported by councils, the rail industry and the Welsh Government.

It works closely with the franchise holders and HOWLTA and works on ongoing promotion of the line, including a detailed website and helping develop the Heart of Wales walking trail.

It developed the Llandeilo Station Hub, a grant aided building that is available for use by local social enterprises and businesses. Currently used on a Friday by the Black Mountain Food Hub, where local food producers deliver their produce in the morning and customers collect their orders in the afternoon, after ordering online.

The hub is hoped to be the first of many across the UK, a sustainable building that provides passenger facilities where stations were bulldozed years ago, and a space for use by community groups and social enterprises.

The opening of the Llandeilo Station Hub

Further possibilities for stations hubs supporting local businesses are being studied, to include a catering trolley service for the line (there is currently no trolley service).

The DevCo has various proposals under development including a cycle hire project for Llandovery and finishing the walking trail in 2019

The Heart of Wales Line Trail

The Heart of Wales Line Trail is a long distance walk that weaves between stations along the line.

The idea came about in 2015 when a group of walkers and rail enthusiasts met in a pub to discuss building a rail-based walking trail from Craven Arms to Llanelli, snaking between stations along the Heart of Wales Line.

The route was explored and landowners consulted, and in January 2017 the steering group launched a crowdfunding appeal to raise money to help build the trail. It received strong support from local communities, walking groups and councils and, with a large input of volunteer labour, the trail is well underway.

The route is based on existing rights of way, starting in the old railway town of Craven Arms and passes through remote upland areas including Shropshire AONB, the Radnorshire Forest, Brecon Beacons and the salt marshes of the Loughor Valley down to the Millennium Coastal Park in Llanelli. It is suitable for long-distance walkers as well as those who wish to walk the trail in sections, using the train to access day or weekend walks and using local, cafés, pubs and overnight accommodation along the way. The completed trail will be over 229 km (142 miles) in length.

At the time of writing the trail is already open across Shropshire, much of Carmarthenshire and the City of Swansea. Full maps and descriptions of the route are available online at www.heart-of-wales.co.uk as well as at several stations.

> "The station at Craven Arms, it was so sad they pulled it down. As the first pickaxes were going into the station I said "what are you going to do with the stone?" "Oh we shall just get rid of it" "Well I'll buy it" Because they were talking, literally, of throwing it all away. And with this we built a wall right round the garden. What's more it hasn't fallen down yet. It's a house that is now called the Manor, Corfton Manor".
>
> *P Cameron*

HOWLTA

The Heart of Wales Line Travellers' Association was formed in 1981, when a group of regular passengers decided to form an organisation to promote the line and act as a voice for its users.
After the inaugural meeting on 7th November 1981, a recruiting drive for members began and the first newsletter came out in early 1982.

Since then the organisation has grown tremendously, with a current membership of over 600, four newsletters a year and strong connections with other community rail organisations and lobbying groups.

It currently acts as a lobbying group for passengers to the franchise holders and the Welsh Assembly in regard to services and improvements, organises regular events, produces four newsletters a year and coordinates the network of station adoption groups on the line.

Members are also eligible for the Heart of Wales Line Railcard, giving a 1/3rd discount on fares for the line.

More information at www.howlta.org.uk

The Prince of Wales and The Duchess of Cornwall cutting the 150th Anniversary vake, Llandovery Station, July 2018. *PA Images*

Further Resources.

Heart of Wales Line website: www.heart-of-wales.co.uk

Heart of Wales Line Traveller's Association: www.howlta.org.uk

Heart of Wales Line Travellers' Association
PO Box 778, Swansea SA4 5BL

The Association of Community Rail Partnerships
https://communityrail.org.uk

Transport for Wales: https://tfwrail.wales   0333 321 1202

Nigel Bird Books. Specialist Railway Bookseller
http://nigelbirdbooks.co.uk
Brynhir, Llwynygroes, Tregaron, Ceredigion. SY25 6PY

All The Stations.
In 2017 Geoff Marshall and Vicki Pipe visited all the stations in Great Britain. You can see their journey on the Heart of Wales Line on YouTube:
Search for: All The Stations Episode 32 Heart of Wales Line

For more on The Heart of Wales Line and other railway subjects visit the author's blog at www.scenebyrail.com

More railway books will be published in 2019.
See the blog and twitter feed (@scenebyrail) for updates.

RANDOMRAILWAYS.COM

@RANDOMRAILWAYS

Photo Credits.

Many thanks to the following photographers and organisations for photographs and other content:

Anthony Birdwood

Jon Critchely

Mike Evans

Stephen Thomas - "kgvuk" on Flickr.com

Roger Joanes on Flickr.com

Dorian Spencer Davies
Images on pages 21 & 46
www.dorianspencerdaviesart.com

Llanwrtyd & District Heritage & Arts Centre:
Postcard Image of Llanwrtd Wells Station

The Radnorshire Society:
excerpts from Transactions of the Radnorshire Society, Vol. 54 (1984) - The Community at Builth Road

The National Library Of Wales:

Photos on pages 11,12,17,21, D.C. Harries Collection

Photos on pages 16,19,33, P Abery

Photos on pages 32 & 41, Geoff Charles,
"A trip on the Central Wales railway line from Llanelli to Shrewsbury July 1st, 1983"

Ordnance Survey maps on pages 25 & 50

Extracts from "The Welshman" newspaper on pages 10, 14 & 15

https://www.library.wales

Archive-images.co.uk: Photos on pages 23,24,41,42

All other photos by the author, unless otherwise stated.
All maps, ephemera etc are from the authors personal collection unless otherwise stated

Bibliography.

Heart of Wales Line Guide
HOWLTA & Kittiwake 2004
ISBN 9781902302331

A Celebration of the Heart of Wales Railway
Nigel & Sue Bird 1993

Portrait of the Central Wales Line
Martin Smith, Ian Allan. 1995
ISBN 9780711 023468

The Central Wales Line
A Doughty, Oxford Publishing Co 1997
ISBN 0860935167

The Central Wales Line
Tom Clift, Ian Allan 1982
ISBN 0711012040

The Illustrated Heart of Wales Line
Rob Gittins & Dorian Spencer Davies
Gomer Press 1985

The Radnorshire Society.
excerts from Transactions of the Radnorshire
Society, Vol. 54 (1984) - The Community at Builth Road

HOWLTA Newsletters, 1990-2018

5 car DMU, Llandeilo. May 1986. *Jon Critchley*

> "It had been a busy market day and my grandfather had sold a lot of pairs of a particularly popular shoe, so we sent off an order to Jennings the wholesalers that night. The last post went at 7.30pm with our order. It cost a penny. The order was sent on the Thursday and arrived in Knighton on the passenger train on the Saturday, just two days later".
>
> *P Middleton*